They Found a Way

Mary Cassatt

By Catherine Scheader

Campus Publications

ℂℙ CHILDRENS PRESS, CHICAGO

TO ED

Cover: Mary Cassatt, 1845-1926. *Young Mother Sewing.*
Oil on canvas. 36¾ x 29 in.
Signed (lower right): Mary Cassatt
The Metropolitan Museum of Art, Bequest of Mrs. H. O. Havemeyer, 1929.
The H. O. Havemeyer Collection.

Frontis: Mary Cassatt, *Portrait of the Artist*
Gouache.
The Metropolitan Museum of Art
Bequest of Edith H. Proskauer, 1975

Library of Congress Cataloging in Publication Data

Scheader, Catherine.
  Mary Cassatt.

  (They found a way)
  SUMMARY: A biography of an American artist whose
many paintings of women and children reveal the influence
of French Impressionism.
  1. Cassatt, Mary, 1844-1926—Juvenile literature.
2. Painters—United States—Biography—Juvenile literature. [1. Cassatt, Mary, 1844-1926. 2. Painters]
I. Title. II. Series.
ND237.C3S3   759.13 [B] [92]   77-7359
ISBN 0-516-01852-3

CHAPTER ONE

Mary Cassatt could sleep no longer. No matter how hard she squeezed her eyes shut, she could not keep out the morning light. Finally she gave up, threw back the light cover, and sprang out of bed.

Why am I trying to go back to sleep anyway? Mary asked herself. It's a waste of time. I can go for a ride.

She dressed quickly, let herself out the back door, and ran lightly down the path, straight to the stable. Holding the door carefully, ready to shift slightly to avoid its creaking sound, she peered into the dim interior. As soon as she slipped inside, she stopped, listening. Someone else was there.

"Mary?"

Mary jumped at the sound of her brother's voice. "Aleck!" she gasped. "You scared me half to death. What are you doing up so early? I thought you'd be in bed all morning after that party last night."

"I did, too," the young man agreed. "But I woke up early and I just couldn't get back to sleep. How about a ride—just like the old days?" Aleck grinned down at his younger sister, glad she was there to share this lovely morning with him.

"I'm going to miss you, Mary," Aleck said as they rode side by side. "I've liked being home in Philadelphia this year, and spending the weekends out here in Chester."

Mary nodded. She would miss him, too. It seemed that as long as she could remember, Aleck had been studying to be an engineer. Years before, their parents had taken the family to Europe so that he could attend a good school before going to engineering college back home in America. Now he was finished. He had graduated from Rensselaer Polytechnic Institute the year before, and was leaving next week to work in Georgia. Last night, the Cassatts had held a party in his honor. Aleck's friends, the sons and daughters of his parent's friends from Philadelphia and Chester County, came to celebrate with them.

Mary had enjoyed the party. She loved the blue and white silk dress and the fancy shoes she had worn. Her hair had been done up and she knew she looked elegant, almost like one of the older girls who laughed and danced with her brother and his friends.

"Mary, tell the truth. Did you have a good time last night?" asked Aleck. "I thought I saw you standing by yourself, once or twice."

"Aleck, I had the best time of my whole life," she cried, her eyes shining with the memory. "But I had to step back every now and then and really take it all in. There was so much to see! All the beautiful gowns, the swirling silk when the girls danced, the music, the lights! It was splendid. I wanted it never to end.

"If I could have made a picture of it, then it would never be over. Aleck, I could make a hundred pictures of it! I don't want to forget any of it."

"You won't, Mary. But there'll be lots of other parties for you from now on. You're really growing up. In a year or two, you'll be living from one party to the next."

Aleck was surprised to see his sister shake her head firmly.

"Not me!" she cried. "Parties are fun, but I couldn't live for them the way your friends do. There's too much else to do!"

"Like what?" Aleck asked, amused. He could see that she was dazzled by the evening before, and thought she would long for more. Mary was such a funny girl sometimes.

"Like painting pictures," Mary answered promptly. "Just look at this fellow here," she said, running her hand along the mane of her horse. "He's so beautiful. Look at the curve of his back. I just ache to put that line on paper. See all the different shades in his coat? If only I could mix colors like that with my paints!" she exclaimed.

Aleck was taken aback by the intensity of his sister's feelings. He had always enjoyed watching her draw and play with her paints, but he did not know how serious she was. He realized that while he had been busy with his own activities, she had been growing in ways that he had not noticed.

"Mary, you're painting better all the time," he said, wanting to encourage her. But she shook her head.

"Not fast enough, Aleck. I'll never get much better until I get some really good training. I have a secret to tell you." Mary turned, and Aleck was amazed at the flash in her eyes. "I'm going to Europe to learn with the best."

"Europe!" Now Aleck was really astonished. He thought he was used to his sister's independence and direct manner. She had been riding with him since her first days on a horse, when they lived year-round in the country, and he loved her spirit. She said what she thought, and he never felt that he had to treat her like a girl. She was more like a younger friend. But this was too much.

"Europe!" he repeated, unable to hide his surprise. "Why Europe?"

"Because the best painting is in Rome and Paris, and that's how you learn to paint really well," Mary said in a rush. "You see the best, try to do it yourself, and learn how."

"But Rome or Paris, Mary? What do you think Father will say?" Aleck asked, gently now, because he knew she was serious.

Some of Mary's confidence vanished at the mention of their father. She bit her lip and took a deep breath.

"It won't be easy, Aleck, but I'll do it. It just means persuading him that this is very important to me."

"He'll never agree," said Aleck, shaking his head. "I don't like to put you down, Mary. But you know, people have some definite ideas about what it is like to be sixteen years old in a family like ours in the year 1860. There is a certain kind of life that Mother and Father have in mind for you. And it doesn't include painting in Europe, I can tell you that."

To Aleck's surprise, Mary just laughed. "Let me describe that life, Aleck. It begins with being introduced into society, studying with Miss So and So to get a little polish in my social bearing, and then having a series of young men from the best families call on me. This wonderful, exciting life will be topped off by a marriage to a young man from a good Philadelphia family. Aleck, I know exactly what they have in mind for me, but it's not what I'm going to do!" She shook her head, frowning again. "You had a chance to study and prepare for your work. Why shouldn't I?"

Aleck didn't know what to say. He began slowly. "Mary, I agree with you. It *isn't* fair, but I don't know what you can do about it. You're a girl, and *that's* what makes it different. They'll let you take drawing lessons with someone nearby, but that's about it, I'm afraid." He knew how much he was hurting her, but he had to be honest with her.

Mary wasn't as troubled as he thought she would be. "I've heard it all before, Aleck. But you're wrong—and you'll see you are. I want to do this more than anything else, and I'll find a way. If I'm good, why should it matter that I'm a girl? Besides, it doesn't mean that I won't have a nice social life, too. I like parties and having fun. I just don't want to do it all my life, and live the life of an idle rich woman. I love my work, and I want the chance to learn how to do it really well.

"The hardest part will be talking Father into it. But I have time. You see, I'm not talking about going tomorrow.

"Come on, Aleck, I'll race you to the oak tree!"

Before Aleck could answer, Mary had slapped the side of her horse, and was out ahead of him. He laughed and started after her. "Maybe you'll do it after all, Mary. If anyone can, you will!" he called, as they raced along. But she was too far ahead to hear him.

CHAPTER TWO

Aleck was right about Mr. Cassatt's reaction to Mary's plans. Mary waited a very long time before asking her father about studying abroad. When at last she did, he wasn't even shocked. He simply would not consider it at all.

"Living alone among all those artists! What an idea!" he said to his wife later. "I thought Mary was growing up, but now I'm not so sure."

His wife listened thoughtfully to Mr. Cassatt. "She *is* growing up, Robert. Mary seems gifted. I know that it's hard for you to imagine a life other than that of a Philadelphia lady for her, but there is more to Mary than to these other young girls we know. Maybe we should give her the chance to express her ideas. She seems to believe in herself so much! I don't want to spoil that in her. If only there was a way to let her study art and still continue her education here."

"Well, I won't consider it, Mother, and the subject is closed. If Mary is so intent on sketching, she can do plenty of it around here."

Mrs. Cassatt did not press the matter. She knew her husband loved each of their children, and enjoyed seeing them develop.

In fact, he was more interested in the family than he was in his business, she reflected with a small sigh that he did not hear. Robert Cassatt did not get deeply into any of the business activities that the rest of his family thrived on. He had only a minor interest in the firm that bore his name, and their income and life-style reflected his limited activity. His nature was restless and he devoted a great deal of time to real estate. As Mr. Cassatt had bought and sold property in Philadelphia and its surrounding area, the family had settled in house after house during the years the children were growing.

Twice, he had taken the whole family for extended visits to Europe, where he seemed more at home. When Aleck showed a flair for engineering, he immediately moved the family to Darmstadt, Germany. There, Aleck attended a school that Mr. Cassatt regarded as the finest preparatory school of its kind.

In spite of herself, Mrs. Cassatt wondered why they couldn't do the same for Mary. It was different, she knew. Mary was a young lady, and that made all the difference! Still, she felt sorry for her daughter, and wanted to help her. They would have to find a way to give her the chance to do what she loved to do, without letting her ruin her life.

Mary half expected her father to refuse her request, and while she was disappointed, she was not discouraged. She knew that it would take time and determination to convince him. During the following months, she spent every spare moment painting, trying to improve her skill. Then she approached her father again about studying art in Paris.

"Mary, honestly, I thought you'd have more sense. How can you talk about leaving when the country's in a war? Do you realize that with the War Between the States going on there's no telling what can happen to Americans in Europe? Come to your senses and be reasonable."

"How about when the war is over?" Mary asked. She was learning how to express her ideas clearly and calmly with her father.

"Who knows when that will be? You should count your blessings and be thankful that you're not living where you're mixed up in it. This is no time to bother me with this nonsense about art."

"But Father, it's very important to me. It's not something I can just forget about. I'm really good. I want to be better, that's all."

Mr. Cassatt was furious with his daughter, and stormed out of the room. Later, he complained bitterly to his wife. "None of the other children are so stubborn. I can't imagine where Mary gets her ideas."

His wife just nodded, and looked away. "Robert, I can't imagine, either. But that isn't helping Mary. She's plainly unhappy. You'll have to think of some way to help her."

The next day, Mr. Cassatt called Mary into his study. Turning to her with a hard look, he demanded, "What would you say to attending the Pennsylvania Academy of the Fine Arts?"

At first, Mary didn't know what to say. It was not what she expected to hear from her father. She needed time to think about it. She knew the building that housed the Academy in the city. It had broad, marble steps and a rare and large hawthorne tree growing in the courtyard. She knew from her friends that the Academy had a section for women, or rather, young ladies. But her heart was sinking. This wasn't Paris! Would she ever get the chance to study there?

"Father," she began haltingly, trying to hold back the tears of disappointment, "that's very generous. May I think about it?" she asked, looking carefully at him. She didn't want to hurt him. She knew that it was difficult for him to offer even this. But she wasn't sure that this was the right thing for her to do. It might delay her ever getting started. She wanted to talk to Aleck. He had returned from Georgia and was working for the Pennsylvania Railroad. Aleck was good to talk to when a problem had to be solved. Maybe he could help her decide.

Aleck saw Mr. Cassatt's offer as a way for Mary to gain advanced training in her field and to provide more time for growing up.

"Look at it this way, Mary," he said. "You're not taking a big step. You can do what you love to do, and yet be close to home while the war is still on. If you decide that it isn't what you want to do with your life, you haven't cut yourself off from everything. If you want to do more, then you can show Father that you're ready. Also, you'll be a little older by then. After all, you're not seventeen yet."

"Aleck, you can be sure of one thing. I won't change my mind about becoming an artist. But maybe you're right. I'll be so good that Father will have to send me to Europe. I'll go to the Academy of Art here and I'll learn everything they'll let me learn.

"Did you know they have a separate section for women?" she asked scornfully.

"That won't bother you, Mary," her brother said softly. "Just be the best."

Mary Cassatt and other students at The Pennsylvania Academy of the Fine Arts.
Inez Lewis, Miss Welch, Eliza Haldeman, Mary Cassatt, and Dr. Edmund Smith.
Photo by Gihon & Rixon, 1024 Chestnut Street, Philadelphia.
Courtesy of The Pennsylvania Academy of the Fine Arts.

CHAPTER THREE

As their horse-drawn carriage approached the white-columned building on Chestnut Street, Lydia Cassatt squeezed her sister's hand.

"We're almost there, Mary," she said, smiling at the younger girl. "Are you excited?"

"A little," Mary admitted, grateful that Lydia was with her. Mary had expected her father to insist on bringing her to the Pennsylvania Academy of the Fine Arts this first day. She was relieved when Lydia offered to come instead. Although she dearly loved him, Mr. Cassatt would have made her uncomfortable today.

Somehow he managed to give the impression, when talking to relatives and friends, that his young daughter would soon outgrow her current interest in art. She certainly didn't want him to give anyone at the Academy that idea!

Soon after Mr. Cassatt proposed the idea of her studying there, Mary received a letter requesting a sample of her work for review by the Committee on Instruction.

It was hard to decide which picture to submit! She lined up her work along a wall of her bedroom, and looked each piece over with a critical eye, trying to guess what the committee would be looking for.

"I can't choose, Lydia," she sighed at last. "The watercolor of the house in West Chester is pretty, but it didn't really turn out the way I wanted it to. The stone work doesn't look real. The still life is all right—I guess. Maybe I should send one of the pencil drawings, like this picture of you. It's a good likeness."

Lydia shook her head at the pencil drawing. She liked the still life best. "It's a fine picture, Mary," she observed. "One of your best. It has a sense of refinement and elegance about it that will be pleasing to the committee."

"Dull," Mary murmured. Although she thought the picture too stiff and formal, she knew that Lydia was probably right. After all, refinement and elegance were qualities that the Academy prized. Moreover, the still life was not glaringly different from her other work.

Despite Lydia's assurances, Mary wavered between self-confidence and concern that her work would seem inadequate to the committee.

"I have so much to learn," she sighed. "I hope I'll find what I need at the Academy."

After Mary received her formal acceptance, she began to look forward to attending classes.

"I'm really excited," she confided to her sister. "This will be the first chance I've had to be with other artists. Even though most of the girls are amateurs, it will be fun to be with people who share my interest."

"Mary, I know you'll like it. I'm so happy that you'll have this chance," Lydia replied.

Mary smiled at her sister. She was grateful for her support this past summer. Aleck was away, working in his new job with the Pennsylvania Railroad.

At the corner of Eleventh and Chestnut Streets, the driver helped the two young women out of the carriage. At the top of the broad marble steps, Lydia turned to her sister. "The last step, Mary," she said. "It's a big one. Do you want me to come in with you?"

Mary laughed and shook her head. "No thanks, Lydia," she said, taking a quick skip through the doorway. "I'm ready for it! See you later!" With a short wave to the older girl, she hurried through the lobby, while Lydia returned to the waiting carriage.

It took Mary only a short time to confirm what she had heard about the Academy. The young women sketching at their easels in the antique classes were from good Philadelphia families like hers. The girls themselves seemed happy to sketch endlessly from the plaster casts of Roman and Greek statues. But Mary quickly discovered another girl who thought as she did.

"I'm going to be an artist, too," announced Eliza Haldeman firmly, when she introduced herself.

Mary was immediately drawn to this cool, confident girl who expressed her determination so easily. The two girls spent long hours in the studio, finishing their sketches after their class-mates went home. They appraised each other's work with the critical eyes of professionals.

"You've got that shadow just right, Eliza," Mary pointed out one day, "but I think the foreshortening on the left arm isn't enough. The way the arm is bent, you've got to crop it a little more, so it doesn't look longer than the outstretched one."

Eliza looked back and forth from the easel to the cast of the Roman warrior, Pericles, with his head turned to one side. She corrected the left arm as Mary suggested.

"How's that?" she asked, as she stepped back at last.

"That's just right," said Mary approvingly.

Eliza wiped the charcoal dust from her fingers and sighed. "You know, Mary, I feel as if we've learned all we can from these casts."

Mary nodded grimly. "We certainly have, Eliza. How I wish we could join a life class! It's not fair to admit only men students to those classes. We can draw as well as they can. What I wouldn't give to draw from a real model! Listening to lectures on anatomy and drawing from these casts is no substitute!"

Eliza waved her arm toward the easels of the other students.

"These girls will be struggling here for a long time, trying to make good drawings of these silly casts. We're far better than any of them now, and yet we'll have to stay here, too, doing the same thing over and over. It doesn't make sense!"

"You're right, Eliza. It's hard to grow when we're not challenged. Well, at least we can look forward to the painting classes. They'll be starting soon."

Eliza groaned. "And, when we're really good, we'll get to copy one of the paintings here at the Academy. What a treat!"

"It's not the copying that I mind," Mary said, frowning thoughtfully. "That's one good way to learn how to paint, I'm convinced."

The other girl nodded in agreement. "I am, too. I just wish we had something better to copy from."

"Some day we will, Eliza!" said Mary with a determined glint in her eye. "When the war is over, I'm going to be at the Louvre in Paris copying from really great pictures! And so will you!"

Mary Cassatt, *Mother and Child.* Pastel.
The Metropolitan Museum of Art
Bequest of Mrs. H.O. Havemeyer, 1929.
The H.O. Havemeyer Collection.

CHAPTER FOUR

Five years later, on board ship, Mary could hardly believe that she was actually on her way to Paris. There were many times during those years when she had almost lost all hope.

And then, one night at dinner, she was startled to hear her father mention the name of a family they'd met years before in Paris. As soon as she heard the name, Mary became alert.

"The last time we heard from them was at Christmas, Robert. What made you think of them?" Mrs. Cassatt asked her husband.

"Because I'm writing to them in the morning. If Mary is going to Paris, she'll need to stay with a good family who lives in a convenient location."

Mary could hardly believe her ears. After all the months of pleading, he was actually starting to make arrangements!

"Aleck tells me that it's not at all unusual for young women to study abroad these days. If Mary has learned all she can in Philadelphia, then it's time she went somewhere else. Since the war ended, three or four ladies from the families of Aleck's friends have done so, I'm told," Mr. Cassatt continued.

"And Eliza Haldeman, Father," Mary added quickly.

"Yes, yes, Mary. I think you've mentioned that before. Well, anyway, I'll write a few letters, and see what we can find out. And if it seems feasible, Mother, what would you say to a vacation in Paris next year? We could get Mary settled there if I can shake loose from the office for a little while."

None of them doubted that Mr. Cassatt would arrange a vacation from his business. He would not miss this opportunity to spend some time in the city he loved best. While Gardner, the youngest Cassatt, stayed with relatives, Lydia, Mary, and their parents set sail.

Her old dream was about to come true, Mary thought as she leaned against the rail of the ocean liner. She was so deep in thought that at first she did not hear her mother's voice beside her.

"I can hardly believe it, Mother! Am I really on my way to France?"

Her mother laughed. "Believe it, Mary. In less than a week, we'll be in Paris."

"There were times, Mother, when I thought Father would never relent!"

"He wants the best for you, Mary. We all do. I just hope this is what you really want."

Mrs. Cassatt looked away, trying to hide her own doubt and confusion. She could not understand how Mary could be so determined to pursue a career in art. None of their friends' daughters had such ambitions. Most of them had already followed the traditional pattern of marriage and motherhood.

Mary suddenly hugged her mother. "I can guess what you're thinking, Mother! 'Why doesn't Mary want to get married instead of studying art?' Tell the truth, isn't that what you're asking yourself, right now?" she teased.

Mrs. Cassatt's cheeks colored. Mary had a direct way of speaking that often caught her off guard. As she tried to think of a reply, her daughter continued.

"Maybe I will marry some day. After all, lots of people aren't married at twenty-two. But right now, I'm sure that painting is something I have to do. None of the young men I've met interests me as much as my work does."

Once in Paris, Mr. Cassatt set about choosing an instructor for Mary. Not one of those wild young men who attracted the easygoing Parisian students to his studio, but an established, good painter with quarters in a quiet neighborhood. A nice, protected environment for a proper young Philadelphia lady would be just right for his Mary.

"Nice, protected, and stifling!" fumed Mary several months later to her friend Walter, another American art student.

"Except for the sights and smells of this city, I might as well be in Philadelphia at the Academy. My teacher, Monsieur Chaplin, is a competent artist, Walter. He's very sure of himself, but *so* academic," she complained. "He has such narrow opinions!

"I told him about a painting by the artist Courbet that I'd seen, and he said really disparaging things about it."

"Academic painters like Chaplin think that Courbet is flashy and vulgar, not worthy of comparison with the artists they like," remarked Walter. "Every now and then, one of those new painters gets a picture into an exhibit here, but you can be sure Chaplin doesn't pay much attention to it!"

"There are only two ways for his students to proceed, his way and the wrong way," grumbled Mary. "I'll bet Eliza's instructor isn't so set in his ways!"

"How is Eliza?" inquired Walter. "I haven't heard you mention her lately."

"I don't see much of her," Mary replied, slowly. "She's living on the other side of the city, working at a studio over there, and in with a crowd of other students. It's hard to keep in touch."

Walter nodded, understanding. He knew that Mary lived a quiet life. The family she was staying with, picked by her parents, kept her close to home.

He smiled at his new friend. Walter liked this elegant young woman with her definite ideas, so different from the American girls he remembered from home. He was going to suggest that she come to his own teacher, but realized that she was looking for more independence.

"Go to the Louvre, Mary!" the young man urged. "You'll find the greatest teachers there."

Mary clapped her hands together. "You know, Walter, that's just what I was thinking!" she said. "I'll tell M. Chaplin that I'm leaving, and then I'll tell Father. He's planning a trip over next year, and by then, I'll have improved so much that he'll know it was the right decision."

For the first time since she came to Paris, Mary felt her heart lift with the feeling that comes from the freedom to choose the way one knows is right.

Before long, Mary's trim, erect figure was a familiar sight in the long, glass-roofed galleries of the Louvre. On either side of her were other students, struggling as she was to learn the secrets of painting and composition from the old masters. Mary did not want to learn to paint like them, but to synthesize their techniques into a style of her own.

Some of the people copying in the Louvre were much older than she was. She knew that many painters continued to copy the masters after they became expert. They made a living from the sale of the copies and made no attempt to do original work.

Visitors to the museum walked slowly among the easels. When the good light was gone, and she'd put her canvas away for the day, Mary toured the galleries, too.

In the commercial galleries around the city, she found herself drawn to contemporary pictures. She began to seek out certain canvases with little-known signatures: Manet and Monet, Pissarro, Cezanne, and Degas. They did unusual things with light, Mary noticed. The way it was used, the light changed colors and forms. She could see that these artists were breaking away from the familiar academic traditions and creating unique ways to express their vision.

Mary's letters home hinted at the excitement being generated by the new painters. The letters she received brought precious news from home.

"My brothers are doing well," she reported to the family with whom she lived. "Aleck's been promoted again to a new job in the railroad and he's going to marry Lois Buchanan. She's a niece of James Buchanan, who was our president before Lincoln. And Gardner's decided on a career in banking. He'll be successful too, I know."

"If they are as dedicated as you are, I can see why they are successful," replied Madame. She admired the young girl who was so committed to her work. She knew that she must be homesick at times, but if she was, Mary showed it only by plunging deeper into her work.

Mary Cassatt, *The Stocking.* Dry point.
The Metropolitan Museum of Art
Bequest of Mrs. H.O. Havemeyer, 1929
The H.O. Havemeyer Collection

CHAPTER FIVE

One morning in 1870, Mary hastily said good-bye to her Parisian hosts. She was sailing for the United States, summoned home by her worried family. France was at war with Prussia, and her safety was a concern. Since the cable had arrived, conditions in Paris had deteriorated even more, and there was word that the city would soon be under siege.

She was sorry to leave. Except for the summer before, when a friend from Philadelphia, Miss Gordon, went south with her on a painting trip to the Italian border, she had worked in Paris steadily for the past four years. Mary had enjoyed the change of scenery on the trip with her friend and was looking forward to another vacation this summer. But now the war made all such trips impossible.

"It will be for only a short time," she assured her friends. "As soon as this war is over, I'll be back. In the meantime, I can visit the family. You know, Aleck and his wife have a son I've never seen. And maybe I can sell some of my paintings!"

At home in Philadelphia, it was good to see the family again. Mary was soon busy painting a portrait of her nephew, Eddie. She knew how pleased her mother was to have her home, and she gladly agreed to a visit with Mrs. Cassatt's family in Pittsburgh. In that western Pennsylvania city, Mary felt the warm welcome of cousins who had followed her progress through Mrs. Cassatt's regular letters.

Pittsburgh was geographically near the Midwest, and her cousins' interests were directed toward that flourishing region, rather than toward the highly developed and sedate East. She listened to their enthusiastic descriptions of Chicago and its growing wealth. Perhaps Chicago would be a good place to sell her paintings, she thought. Her cousins Minnie and Aleck Johnson thought so too, and they offered to go there with her.

Mary looked forward to seeing that modern city and meeting the influential Potter Palmer and his wife, who were friends of Aleck. But Mary never met the Palmers. Shortly after she arrived in Chicago, a blazing fire swept out of control, destroying buildings and leaving hundreds homeless. The Great Chicago Fire put an abrupt end to Mary's plans. The three cousins had to leave their hotel in the middle of the night and find safety in another part of the city. Although they escaped injury, the paintings were lost.

With her pictures gone, Mary became anxious to end her visit home and return to Europe. She was grateful that this time her parents were reconciled to her leaving. Their respect for her as a serious, professional artist helped to overcome some of their concern for her safety. She reassured them that she would not go immediately to Paris, which was still rebuilding after the calamity of war. There was much to see in Italy and Spain, she told her family. She would have a chance to visit the great museums in those countries and to learn the lessons of their master painters.

The Cassatts were soon receiving letters from Mary postmarked Rome and Parma, Italy. She wrote to them about the paintings of Correggio, who had painted infants in such a lifelike way that one could almost feel them breathe.

Meanwhile, Paris was gradually restored. Friends there wrote to her when the celebrated annual exhibition, known as the Salon, was revived. Mary submitted a painting, and was thrilled when it was accepted.

In her years in Paris, she had learned about the power and prestige of the Salon. A jury of forty men was selected to decide which paintings would be hung in the exhibit, which was held each year in the Palais de Beaux Arts.

Mary knew that it was almost a necessity for an artist to be accepted at the Salon before gaining any other kind of recognition. To be awarded a ribbon or honorable mention brought almost immediate profit, in terms of selling paintings.

She also knew that Salon jurists were notorious for choosing conservative pictures. They reflected the prevailing taste for classical subjects in stiff, formal poses, or, if the pictures had outdoor subjects, for unreal-looking, romanticized backgrounds.

The modern paintings that she was beginning to prefer were usually ignored. Pictures of ordinary people in relaxed, natural poses were rarely seen at the Salon; nor were paintings, shimmering with light, that had obviously been painted out-of-doors.

Mary hoped the Salon would reflect these new trends one day. Popular taste would change and jurors would become better educated.

In the meantime, her heart beat quicker each time she remembered that one of her own pictures would hang that year in the Salon.

After studying the paintings of the great El Greco and Goya in Spain, Mary went to Antwerp, where she absorbed the techniques of Hals and Rubens, Belgium's noted artists.

She was taking a slow, roundabout way back to Paris, but the trip was deliberate and purposeful. Mary came back to the city she loved enriched by her travels and study.

CHAPTER SIX

Mary returned to Paris in 1873. By then, her adopted city was her real home. She felt comfortable among her artist friends, who knew and appreciated her work. Every year between 1872 and 1876, a picture of hers was accepted at the annual Salon. She moved more and more confidently among her colleagues as her work gained increased recognition.

One day in 1877, an artist friend of Mary's came to see her. He brought with him Edgar Degas, the celebrated painter, whose work Mary admired. She had heard that Degas was a cold and unfriendly person, and she did not know what to expect as she invited the two men in. If he was an unpleasant person, she thought, his appearance did not give him away. Degas was dignified and well dressed, with the formal manners of a gentleman. His eyes hinted at a kind and generous nature. Ten years older than she, he recognized her as a fine artist.

"I've been looking forward to meeting you for a very long time, Mademoiselle Cassatt," said Degas, bowing. "Some years ago, I saw a picture of yours at the Salon, a portrait of a red-haired lady. It was remarkable! I knew that you were an artist who thought as I did."

"It must have been Ida's portrait," replied Mary, delighted with Degas' praise. "My friend Madame Cordier posed for that picture. It hung in the Salon of 1874 and it gave me the courage to submit two pictures the following year. One of them was accepted, but the other was rejected because the jurors thought it was too bright." Mary grimaced in annoyance, remembering that when she toned down the coloring in her portrait of Lydia, and submitted it the following year, it was accepted.

Degas smiled sympathetically. "The jurors at the Salon have their own taste in these matters," he commented ruefully. "And have you submitted anything this year?"

"My latest picture was turned down," Mary replied firmly, without a trace of regret. "I won't change *this* painting!" she added, emphatically. "For five years, I've exhibited in the Salon and that's enough for me. It's been gratifying, but I've outgrown it. The jurors are positively reactionary! They don't change or grow, and I refuse to submit to their evaluation any longer!"

Degas was enchanted with Mary's direct and strong-minded ways. Salon juries *were* narrow and old-fashioned. The circle of painters in which he moved agreed with Mary.

Mary Cassatt, *Portrait of Madame Cordier.* 1874.
Oil on panel. 18¾ x 15¾ in.
Private Collection.

Have you heard of the Independents, Mlle. Cassatt?'' he asked. Mary, who was pouring tea, stopped, electrified.

"Have I!" she exclaimed. "They're my heroes! Their work is alive and exciting! I think it's tragic that the public doesn't know them better. Uninformed critics have hurt them badly. Wasn't it a critic who gave them the name 'Impressionists' after seeing Monet's *Impression Sunrise,* and not understanding it?''

"I'd like you to meet these artists, Mlle. Cassatt," Degas continued. "We no longer tolerate the tyranny of Salon juries each year. Instead, we exhibit independently."

Mary had been to exhibitions by the Impressionists, or Independents, as they preferred to be called. Several of the painters, sculptors, and engravers in the group she knew slightly. After her meeting with Degas, she met them more frequently. Later, she would exhibit with them herself.

Meanwhile, she and Degas became close friends, drawn together by a mutual respect for each other's art. Mary visited Degas' studio almost daily. She watched fascinated as his unusual pictures developed before her eyes. He painted people as they were, and did not idealize them as the academic painters did. His ballet pictures provided glimpses into the backstage life of the dancers, rather than just showing them in familiar on-stage poses. When he came to her studio, he helped by showing her where her strengths were, and by suggesting technical improvements. Although Mary was aware of his influence on her work, she continued to develop a style that was very much her own. Unlike Degas and the other Impressionists who also influenced her, she modeled her figures vigorously, so that their features and expressions were clearly evident.

As is the case in many deep relationships, the friendship between the two artists was not altogether sunny. As she grew to know him, Mary learned how Degas had earned his reputation for making caustic remarks. In his enthusiasm for excellence, he often disregarded her feelings. Sometimes his criticism could be ruthless, but Mary was independent enough not to take it personally.

The two were compatible intellectually as well as artistically. They enjoyed long discussions about the French literature and politics that fascinated her. She was accustomed to expressing her opinions forthrightly, and as they exchanged views, sometimes sharply, Degas became used to her unwavering positions.

CHAPTER SEVEN

In addition to her first meeting with Degas, the year 1877 was critical for Mary Cassatt for another reason. For several years, her father had given less and less attention to his brokerage house. With his sons Aleck and Gardner well established in life, and Mary so independent, his responsibilities had diminished.

On her last visit to Paris the year before, Mary's sister Lydia had speculated about the possibility of Mr. Cassatt's complete retirement.

"Father really wanted to come with me this time," she told Mary. "He must have said it ten times! Not only that, but he asked a great many questions about my last trip here—about prices for carriages and food, for instance. Things that he usually doesn't bother about! He remarked that one could still live quite simply, but well, in Paris. I actually believe he's giving some thought to moving us over here."

"You may be right, Lydia," Mary agreed. "He's always loved Paris. The last time he and Mother came over, he enjoyed himself so much that I thought they might stay then! He told me it wouldn't be long before he retired, and that Paris was the best place in the world in which to live out one's old age."

After that conversation with Lydia, Mary was not surprised to receive a letter early in 1877 from her father, telling her of his plans to move to Paris. While she began looking for a place large enough for them all to live in, Mr. Cassatt arranged for his retirement from the Philadelphia brokerage house of Lloyd and Cassatt. That fall, with arrangements completed on both sides of the Atlantic, he and Mrs. Cassatt, with Lydia, joined Mary in Paris.

Mary immediately felt the change made by the arrival of her family. Their presence altered her life, as she combined a commitment to work with family obligations. The care and attention that her parents expected frequently took her from painting, but Mary's determination and need to create overcame these difficulties. Somehow, she found a way to integrate work into her new life-style.

How could it be any other way? she asked herself. Although her work had originally brought her to France, far from her family, she still felt very close to them.

From the perspective of Mary's recognition as an artist, the great disadvantage of this new arrangement is clear. During the next eighteen years, she did not visit America. At the time the Cassatts settled in Paris, Mary was just gaining maturity as an artist. But the modern French art style in which she painted was not yet well known in America. Mary did her best to reach the American art-buying public during that time. She sent pictures to Aleck, which he showed to his friends and sometimes sold to dealers. Others were submitted to exhibitions in Philadelphia and New York. Later, she dealt directly with galleries in those cities. Unfamiliar with her style, many American dealers did not attend to her paintings as they should have. In any case, it was less effective for others to handle her work than for her to do it herself. As a result, for many years this great painter was unknown among her native countrymen.

Meanwhile, the Cassatt family's life settled into a routine. Mr. Cassatt fussed over his wife and daughters, but left the responsibility for much of the household and family management to Mary. She maintained a balance between domestic demands and professional pressures. Mary knew that Mr. Cassatt's retirement funds were not large, and although Aleck helped the family by providing some of the comforts they could not otherwise afford, they lived simply. Mary paid for studio and models from the sale of her paintings. Busy as it kept her to promote her work with the art dealers, she was pleased to be able to take care of her share of the expenses.

Each summer, the Cassatts traveled to the country. For the first two years, they stayed at resort hotels. After that, Mary decided to rent a villa.

"It will be easier for me to paint," she told her parents, "and more comfortable for all of us."

The arrangements were certainly more complicated than they had been for that first vacation trip she made with Miss Gordon, she realized. But it was worth it to have the change of background for her work, and to know that her mother and sister had the country air to enjoy. She wished her father were as

easily pleased. He was as restless as ever, impatient to return to Paris almost before they were unpacked for the summer.

The Cassatts continued the same kind of social life in France that they had enjoyed at home, and often entertained visiting relatives and friends from Pennsylvania. While this also impinged on Mary's time, she was glad to see her parents happy and occupied.

In spite of these social commitments, Mary continued her close friendship with Degas. He shared with her his plans to publish an art journal, and she contributed an engraving for the first issue. Like several of her paintings and pastels, the engraving had an opera theme. Degas did an etching of Mary herself for the first issue. Though the journal was delayed many times and was never actually published, Degas' etching was preserved. Mary consoled herself with the fact that she had had the opportunity to work once more with engraving plates. It was a skill she had first acquired on her trip to Parma, years earlier.

Degas and Mary frequently went about the city together. At the same time, she became friendly with the other Impressionists. When they invited her to contribute to their annual exhibit in 1879, she felt a special glow at being accepted by the artists whose work she respected so much. Mary chose *La Loge,* a favorite painting with a theater setting. It showed a young girl with brightly colored hair and glowing complexion, dressed in an elegant gown. Behind her were the sweeping curves of the balcony rows. Mary included all the rich colors and familiar

Mary Cassatt. *Lydia dans la loge.*
Oil on canvas. 31⅝ in. h. x 23 in. w.
Private Collection, Philadelphia.

details which made her paintings so appealing. She was pleased that her family was there to share the good notices she received from the critics. Through her Impressionist friends, she heard that the celebrated painter, Paul Gauguin, was impressed with the picture. At the exhibit, he was overheard saying that here was a painter with "much power."

The Impressionists' exhibition of 1879 was a success, both esthetically and commercially. Critics praised the overall quality of the works, and many of them were sold. Mr. Cassatt wrote home to Aleck and Gardner about Mary's growing popularity as an artist.

As time passed, life in the Cassatt household assumed a rhythm of its own. Each spring, there was the frantic work of preparing pictures for hanging in the Impressionists' exhibition. Following the exhibition and its dismantling, the family went to the rented villa in the country where they stayed until the weather changed in October. Mary relaxed, rode horseback, and painted outdoors all summer.

In 1880, Mary's routine was interrupted by the arrival of her brother Aleck, his wife Lois, and their four children, who took a long vacation in Europe. They stayed at a hotel in Paris, near the Cassatts. For Mary, it was a chance to paint the children's pictures. She was able to coax them to pose for her while their parents toured and shopped.

Mary Cassatt. *Mother and Child.* ca. 1890
Oil on canvas. 35⅜ in. h. x 25⅜ in w.
Courtesy of the Wichita Art Museum:
Roland P. Murdock Collection

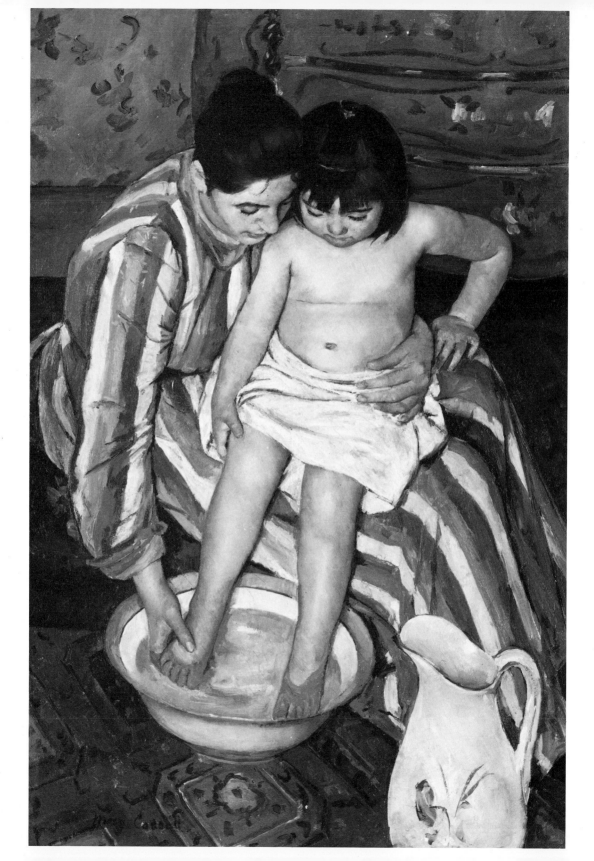

This opportunity to combine travel with a family gathering was very appealing to Aleck. Mary was happy that her brother had the means to enjoy such a life. Aleck and Lois determined that it would be only the first of many trips to Europe. Two years later, when he retired as vice-president of the Pennsylvania Railroad, the family returned once more. After that, they were in Europe almost every second year.

These visits gave Mary a chance to encourage her brother's interest in French painting. She urged him to begin collecting as an investment. Not sure of his own taste, he usually followed her advice in selecting pictures. Mary hoped he would become more interested, since it would be easier for her to purchase pictures for him. But for Aleck, racehorses were of more interest than art. In addition, his wife did not share his even moderate enthusiasm for collecting.

The year 1882 brought a fateful, but not altogether unexpected, change in the Cassatts' life. Lydia, who had not been well for many years, became seriously ill. As her condition grew worse, Mary brought her back to Paris from the country during the summer. By fall, when hope for Lydia's recovery waned, Mary cared for her almost constantly. Even after a nurse was hired at the doctor's insistence, Mary stayed at her side.

When Lydia died in November, it was a great loss to her sister. Neither woman had married, and they had remained very close to each other. During the years when Mary was in Europe by herself, Lydia had been a frequent visitor, either alone or with her parents. Her appearance is familiar to us because of the many paintings in which she was Mary's model.

When Aleck arrived with his family in Paris three weeks later, he could see how deeply affected his sister was by Lydia's death. As she had when they were younger, Mary turned to her older brother for support.

"Aleck, I'm so glad you're here," said Mary. "What a comfort your children will be for Mother and Father, especially this Christmas."

Aleck and Mary talked long into the night about their sister, turning over memories from childhood in an attempt to lessen their sadness.

Then Aleck turned the conversation to Mary's work. "What work?" she asked. "I haven't touched a canvas since early in the summer. I haven't the heart for it, Aleck. Either I'm with Mother and Father these days, or I ride in the park."

"You'll work again, Mary," he assured her. "Each day, it will become easier. With Lois and me here, and the children, you'll have some help with Mother and Father.

"Did you know that the children argue about which of them is the best model for Aunt Mary? They'll be terribly disappointed if you don't get them to pose for you.

"Incidentally," he continued, "we've all been following the notices that you and your Impressionist friends have received in the newspapers. Father sends us all the clippings. I'm looking forward to seeing Monsieur Degas and the others while we're here."

"There's been a quarrel, Aleck, as you've probably heard. Did you know that Degas and I didn't exhibit with the Impressionists this past year? But I'll tell you about it another time. I'm exhausted, and for the first time in weeks, I think I'll sleep the night through. Your being here has already made such a difference!"

Mary Cassatt. *Feeding the Ducks.* Color Etching.
Metropolitan Museum of Art.
Bequest of Mrs. H.O. Havemeyer, 1929.
The H. O. Havemeyer Collection.

CHAPTER EIGHT

The dissension Mary mentioned to Aleck that night had actually begun the year before. In 1881, a chronic dispute among the independent artists became acute.

Mary heard about the crisis from Degas when he called one day at her studio. At first, she did not notice her friend's agitation. She was absorbed in putting the finishing touches on a painting begun the previous summer at Marly, before Aleck's family went home after their first trip.

"Well, what do you think?" she asked him, stepping back and looking critically at the canvas.

As soon as she asked the question, she regretted it. Often, he was franker than he need be. She appreciated his criticism and attributed much of her growth as an artist to his suggestions, but he could be cruel.

She waited now for his answer, daring only to glance sidewise at him. But, although she could sense his uneasiness, he looked long and lovingly at the picture.

"Sublime!" he replied at last. "You've captured your mother's composure perfectly. And the children almost breathe. No one paints children as you do, Mary."

Mary was relieved. She liked the picture too. She had coaxed Katherine, Robert, and Elsie to pose, listening to Mrs. Cassatt read from a book of fairy tales. It was hard for them to sit still, she knew. Especially little Robert, who, despite his own pleasure in painting and drawing, was particularly restless. Mrs. Cassatt often scolded him.

"When you're grown up and an artist yourself, Robert, you'll realize the trouble you gave your poor aunt whenever you sat for a picture with her."

But Mary really didn't mind. The vitality which made it so hard for the children to sit still was what made them such good subjects. She kept a little treasure chest of books and candy nearby to break up long sittings.

Mary added a final brush stroke and turned all of her attention to her friend. Something was clearly wrong, she was certain. He was silent, and frowning more than usual.

"Tell me what's new," she prompted.

"I'm furious with Monet and Renoir!" he blurted out.

So that was it! As soon as she heard the names, she could anticipate the cause of his outrage.

"The same thing again, is it?" she murmured, shaking her head. "They're exhibiting at the Salon, I suppose?"

Degas nodded his head angrily. "After all we've said about entering juried shows! I can't understand them!"

"Now, Edgar," she said gently, "you and I won't submit our work to the Salon or other exhibits that make awards, but you know that everyone doesn't agree with us.

"I'm afraid that our friends Monet and Renoir have some need to enter the Salon that we don't understand. Who knows why? Maybe it's the early ridicule that Monet experienced. The critics were very cruel to him, years ago."

"It hasn't been easy for anyone!" Degas snapped. "But the rest of us have some pride."

Mary could not argue with him. She knew that some of their friends did not sell many pictures, and could use all of the exposure they were offered. However, they maintained their boycott of the Salon. They had little faith in the competence and objectivity of art juries.

Mary sighed and said, "There's not much we can do about it. We've discouraged them in every way we can."

She was puzzled by Degas' ire, since the quarrel was an old one. When he did not reply, but lapsed into another silence, she prodded him a little more.

"You've spoken to them today?" she inquired.

"Yes, and they're not going to change their minds. What's more, they're angry with *us* for encouraging newcomers to join our group! What do you think of that?"

This was different! Mary was told that Monet and Renoir were displeased with some of the younger artists whom she and Degas had befriended. These new artists were not, in fact, Impressionists. Their work represented a diversity that was the natural outcome of creativity.

Mary couldn't help but laugh at the irony of it. "So!" she mused, slowly shaking her head in disbelief. "The former champions of change want no further change. Now, only Impressionists are artists! Remember when it was only academics? This whole episode would be amusing if it weren't so sad, Edgar.

"Well, I believe they're wrong," she continued, with firmness. "And I know you do, too. Others may not call us Independents, but that is what we truly are. And so there must be some acceptance of ourselves as independent thinkers. How I wish Monet and Renoir could see that!"

Although those on both sides of the dispute felt strongly about their respective beliefs, the artists patched up their differences temporarily and the sixth Impressionist exhibit, held in 1881, was a success. Mary's paintings received favorable comments from the critics.

But the squabbling about who should show at the annual exhibits continued, and the next year, 1882, Degas would not enter the exhibit when the group refused to accept his friends. Mary knew just what to do when she heard the news. Degas was her best friend among the artists, and she also withdrew.

"The seventh Impressionist exhibition can open without us both," she told him.

It would be several years before the Impressionists would organize another exhibit and when they did, in 1886, it was the eighth and last such showing. Mary and Degas rejoined the group that year.

Mary never changed her mind about juried exhibitions. She consistently refused invitations to enter her work in them, even when she could have enhanced her reputation by doing so. Later, when her fame spread to America, she declined the honor of being a member of several such juries.

Meanwhile, the rebellion in 1881 drew Mary and Degas closer together. Sometimes they painted together, either at her studio or at his. That same year, she posed for a picture of his, *At the Milliners,* when the model found the pose too difficult.

Degas, Edgar Hilaire Germain. *At the Milliner's.* 1882.
Pastel on paper. 30 in. h. x 34 in. w.
The Metropolitan Museum of Art. Bequest of Mrs. H.O. Havemeyer, 1929.
The H. O. Havemeyer Collection.

CHAPTER NINE

Having Aleck's family with them made the Christmas of 1882, the first one without Lydia, more bearable for Mary and her parents. Just as her brother had predicted, Mary became accustomed to her loss and returned to work. She did a portrait of Aleck that was completed before he and the family sailed for home in April.

Later that same year, their younger brother Gardner arrived in Paris with his bride, Jenny. At the end of their visit, Mary and her mother went to England with the young couple to see them off for home.

While in London, they were lavishly entertained by Mrs. Cassatt's cousin, Mrs. Mary Riddle, and her daughter, Annie Scott. Mary wanted to return the hospitality of the two ladies by painting a portrait of Mrs. Riddle for her daughter. She planned the composition carefully. In the foreground, she placed a Japanese tea set. She posed Mrs. Riddle in the center, wearing a

Mary Cassatt. *Lady at the Tea Table.*
Oil on canvas. 29 in. x 24 in.
Signed and dated (lower left): Mary Cassatt
Metropolitan Museum of Art. Gift of the artist, 1923.

dark dress with a delicate lace cap. The figure is strong, but balanced by the shapes of the tea set.

Mary was pleased with the results. Degas came over to see it, and praised it as one of her best pictures.

"You've painted the face with great delicacy," he said approvingly. "And the blues—they're perfect! The tea set picks up the same shade in the eyes. She's a handsome woman, your mother's cousin."

Mary was pleased with Degas' approval. He usually said what he thought about her paintings, even when his opinion was not complimentary. If he said it was good, she knew he liked it.

Mrs. Cassatt seemed unenthusiastic, even apprehensive, about the picture, and Mary was puzzled.

"You heard M. Degas, mother. It's a work of art, he said."

"I'm sure it's a fine painting, Mary," the older woman said soothingly. "Your friend is a better judge of art than I am. But Annie is a little like me, I'm afraid. She likes a good picture, but for a portrait of her mother, she will expect something that is—well—a little more flattering. Annie and her mother aren't artists, you know."

Although Mary could not agree, she eyed the picture more critically and decided to have it framed before presenting it to Mrs. Scott. "Sometimes a handsome frame can be appealing to a person who isn't sure about his taste in pictures," she remarked.

"Well, we'll see," said Mrs. Cassatt, still doubtful, but not wanting to hurt Mary's feelings any further.

As it turned out, Mrs. Cassatt was correct. Mrs. Scott made polite comments about the portrait at first, but then mentioned the nose. Wasn't it a bit too large? she wondered.

Mary felt let down. Not a word about the quality of the painting—the colors, the balance, the technique. It was hard to please other people! Mary consoled herself that she was not a portrait painter. This painting had been an exception. She painted to please herself and her own esthetic standards.

Mrs. Scott did not take the picture with her, hoping, no doubt, that Mary would redo the part that was displeasing to her. Mary put it away, undecided about what to do and disappointed that her gift had been rejected. She thought of it as a gift of herself to the women she liked so much. In time, the picture was put deeper into storage and forgotten until many years later, after Mrs. Cassatt and Mrs. Riddle were both dead.

Mary's friend, art connoisseur Louisine Elder, then Mrs. Henry O. Havemeyer, discovered the painting in 1914, and had Mary's art dealer display it. The public confirmed Mary's and Degas' early opinion of the picture.

While Mary's paintings received the approval of her colleagues and enjoyed critical acclaim in France, they were not always understood by the conventional people of Philadelphia, or even by her own family. The story of Mrs. Riddle's portrait is a good example of their reactions.

Today, the portrait is in the collection of the Metropolitan Museum of Art in New York, a gift from Mary. The strong outline and colors attract one's attention to this beautiful painting.

Mary Cassatt. *Portrait of a Young Girl.*
Oil on canvas. 29 in. x 24⅛ in.
The Metropolitan Museum of Art.
Anonymous Gift, 1922.

CHAPTER TEN

By the time the Impressionists exhibited together for the last time in 1886, their art was known in America, due largely to the influence of Mary Cassatt.

Although she was not in her native land between the years 1872 and 1890, she was instrumental in arousing interest there in the work of her adopted countrymen. The first Impressionist paintings that came to America were from two sources: Aleck Cassatt and Mary's friend, Louisine Elder Havemeyer.

Aleck's interest in art was relatively mild, due perhaps to his wife's disinterest and his greater enthusiasm for racehorses. Mary was more effective with Louisine Elder. Their friendship, begun in a chance meeting years earlier, influenced what would become a great collection of European art in America.

When Mary returned to Paris in 1873 after her trip to America and her travels through Italy, Spain, and Belgium, she made a brief call on a friend who conducted a boarding school for young girls.

She could not stay, as she was on her way to Courbet's studio to see a painting he had just completed. Mary chatted for a few minutes about Courbet and the other artists she knew.

Timidly at first, one of the American girls began to ask questions about the artists. Pleased with the teen-ager's interest and intelligence, Mary promised to take Louise Elder to an art gallery, where she could see for herself the works of the Impressionists.

Later, she helped Louise buy her first painting, a small pastel by Degas. It cost one hundred dollars, Louise's entire allowance for the year. The young girl was very excited about her purchase, which was the first picture in what would become the great Havemeyer collection.

With Mary's help, Louise bought other French paintings before she returned to America. When she married Henry O. Havemeyer and changed her name to Louisine, she and her husband continued to collect pictures. They brought to America the first examples of French Impressionist art.

Louisine, her husband, and Mary remained close friends. On their trips to Europe, the Havemeyers visited Mary and traveled with her to the art centers of the continent. Mary helped them discover unusual values and advised them on additions to their collection.

The Havemeyers lived in New York City, which was a more sophisticated art center than Philadelphia. Mary herself sent many of her paintings to New York, where they were more readily accepted than in her home city.

As the years passed, inevitable changes took place in Mary's life. A fall from her horse in 1888 ended her pleasure in riding. She had loved horses and riding since her childhood, when she

Mary Cassatt. *Nurse Reading to a Little Girl.* 1895.
Pastel on paper. 23¾ in. x 28⅞ in.
The Metropolitan Museum of Art.
Gift of Mrs. Hope Williams Read, 1962.

Mary Cassatt. *Fillette au Chapeau.* Dry Point.
The Metropolitan Museum of Art.
Rogers Fund, 1919.

and Aleck rode together through the Pennsylvania countryside. As soon as the income from the sale of her paintings permitted, she had bought a horse and rode him regularly until the accident. Her injury ended an activity that Mary loved and she always missed it.

In 1891, her father died. Mr. Cassatt had lived to see his daughter's work recognized on two continents, and to see her support herself comfortably.

In the year after Mr. Cassatt's death, Mary was invited to paint three decorative panels for the Women's Building at the Chicago World's Fair. At first, she had misgivings about the project. The large scale required was not a comfortable one for her to work in. Moreover, she had never done a mural before.

While she was trying to decide whether to accept the invitation, her mother suggested asking Degas' opinion. Mary emphatically refused. Their relationship had been strained frequently during the years, and they were presently not on the best of terms. Also, Mary was sure that he would discourage her for the very same reasons that made her hesitate. He would not see the advantages that she did.

Mary saw the project as an opportunity to celebrate feminine contributions to modern life. Moreover, she was keenly aware of her unusual role as a successful artist who was also a woman. That too, was something to celebrate. Perhaps some talented young woman would come to the building, see Mary Cassatt's murals, and say to herself, A woman painted those. If she can be an artist, so can I.

Having been away from America so long, Mary knew how little known her work was in her native country. Thousands of people who would not go to a museum or an art gallery would go to the Fair and see her work for the first time.

Once Mary made up her mind to accept the contract, she set to work seriously on the project. The work would be done at the summer house she and her mother had rented. The size of the paintings was a problem. To overcome the difficulty of painting the top of the large panels, she had a narrow trench dug into which she lowered each panel after she completed the bottom part. In this way, she was able to paint the upper portion without the need for a ladder. The painting area was roofed with glass, so that she could leave the canvasses in place until they were finished.

Mary painted a wide border around each panel, which reduced the area in which she painted her pictures. Within the border, she painted almost life-size pictures of women in modern dress, symbolically pursuing the arts, knowledge, and fame.

The project was even more difficult than she had anticipated. All kinds of misunderstandings occurred. After she worked out the scale and began painting, the exhibit director sent dimensions of the area where the works would be. Even more disap-

Mary Cassatt. *Woman with a Dog.*
In the Collection of the Corcoran Gallery of Art.

Mary Cassatt. *The Straw Hat.* ca. 1899. Dry Point.
The Metropolitan Museum of Art.
Bequest of Mrs. H. O. Havemeyer, 1929.

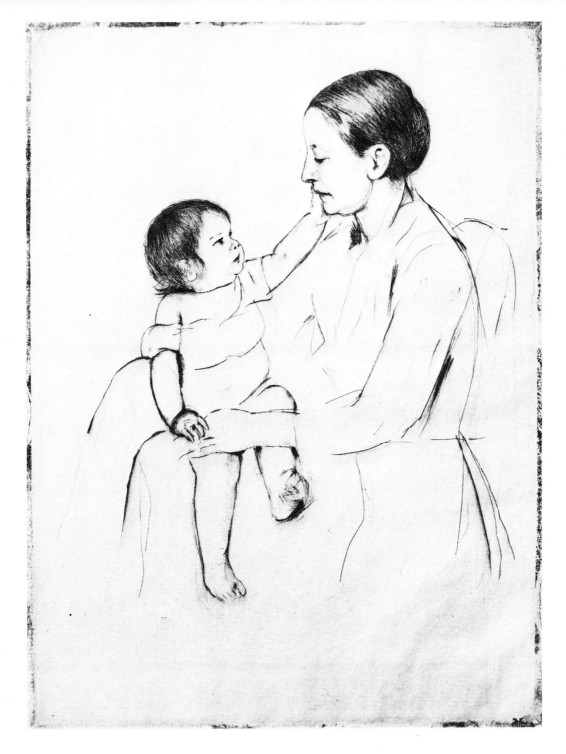

Mary Cassatt. *La Caresse.* Dry Point. Dated: 1891
The Metropolitan Museum of Art.
Gift of Arthur Sachs, 1916.

pointing was the height at which they were hung. Many of the lovely details that Mary had worked on so painstakingly would be lost to view.

The murals at the Chicago World's Fair were only one sign of the increasing recognition Mary was beginning to receive. She had one-woman shows and sold many prints and pastels as well as paintings. She continued to grow as an artist, adapting her style to new discoveries she made about light, form, and color.

A Japanese influence came into her work following an 1890 Japanese art exhibition in Paris. Mary began to incorporate strong patterns contrasting with flat, solid surfaces in her paintings. Her prints demonstrated a strong linear sense, another indication of the Japanese style.

In 1895, Mary's mother died, and for the first time in eighteen years, no member of Mary's family was with her in France. She was free to travel and did so, not only to other parts of the continent, but also to the United States.

The Havemeyer's took her with them to Italy and Spain. Mary scouted out rare and beautiful old paintings for them. It was an exciting trip for Henry and Louisine. In Parma and Rome Mary shared with them her favorite Italian painters. In Spain they bought El Grecos and Goyas. Mary had the flair and patience to find exactly the right paintings for the Havemeyers.

Mary Cassatt. *Maternal Caress.* 1891.
Dry point, soft-ground etching, and aquatint, third state;
Printed in color; from a series of ten. 14⅜ in. x 10⁹⁄₁₆ in.
The Metropolitan Museum of Art.
Gift of Paul J. Sachs, 1916.

Mary Cassatt. *The Letter.* 1891.
Dry point, soft-ground etching, and aquatint, third state;
Printed in color; from a series of ten. 13⅝ in. x 8¹⁵⁄₁₆ in.
The Metropolitan Museum of Art.
Gift of Paul J. Sachs, 1916.

Mary Cassatt. *Women Bathing.* 1891.
Dry point, soft-ground etching, and aquatint, fifth state;
Printed in color; from a series of ten. 14⁵⁄₁₆ in. x 10⁹⁄₁₆ in.
The Metropolitan Museum of Art.
Gift of Paul J. Sachs, 1916.

In her later success, Mary never forgot her struggles as a young artist. She became president of the Art League in Paris, which sheltered American students. She sponsored scholarships, but made it a requirement that the students copy the masters for a year.

Long after her close association with the Impressionist painters ended, she continued to decline prizes, and refused to serve on juries that judged other artists' work.

Her old age was saddened by the death of her brothers, Aleck and Gardner, and her old friend, Degas. Mary's eyesight gradually failed and she developed cataracts in both eyes. By 1914, she could paint no longer. During the last twelve or fourteen years of her life, she was isolated from the work she loved.

A misunderstanding about some prints caused a serious quarrel with Louisine Havemeyer, and Mary, even more strong-minded and irritable in her old age than previously, refused to write to her old friend.

Her only companion was the servant Mathilde, who had worked for her and her parents for many years. She was with Mary until she died in 1926, at the country house she owned at Beaufresne in the south of France.

Because of her election years earlier to the Legion of Honor, France honored Mary Cassatt with an imposing burial ceremony

Mary Cassatt in front of the Villa Angeletto, Grasse, 1912.
Courtesy of the Art Institute of Chicago.

which included military honors. Her neighbors from Beaufresne filled the church with roses, Mary's favorite flower.

At her death, Philadelphia gave her the praise it had often withheld during her lifetime. The *Philadelphia Inquirer* said she was considered by critics on two continents to be one of the best women painters of all time.

Mary's paintings are a rich legacy to all of us. During her lifetime, museums tended to ignore her paintings, and many of them found their way instead into private collections. As time passed, many of Mary's paintings were willed to museums. Now, in almost every large city in America, you can go into its museum of art and find at least one Mary Cassatt painting, usually in a collection donated by a benefactor who years ago recognized the genius of this great painter.

When you look at those paintings, you can see the beautiful forms and glowing colors of Mary Cassatt's unique vision. Let your eyes dim a little, and you will almost feel that you are sitting across the room from the lady with the cup of tea, or standing in the yard with that girl squinting in the sun, under her big straw hat. A hundred years later, they continue to grace our lives with beauty because a young woman took hold of the gift she had, dreamed of developing that gift, and found a way to make her dream a reality.

Mary Cassatt. *A Cup of Tea.*
Oil on canvas. 36⅜ in. x 25¾ in.
The Metropolitan Museum of Art.
Anonymous Gift, 1922.

BIBLIOGRAPHY

Breeskin, Adelyn D., *Mary Cassatt, A Catalogue Raisonne of the Oils,
Water-Colors, and Drawings,* Washington: Smithsonian Institution Press, 1970.
Carson, Julia M. H. , *Mary Cassatt,* New York: David McKay Co., 1966.
Hale, Nancy, *Mary Cassatt,* Doubleday & Company, Inc. Garden City,
New York, 1975.
Havemeyer, Louisine W., *Sixteen to Sixty, Memoirs of a Collector,* New York:
Metropolitan Museum of Art, 1930.
Sweet, Frederick A., *Miss Mary Cassatt, Impressionist from Pennsylvania,*
Norman: University of Oklahoma Press, 1966.
Wilson, Ellen, *American Painter in Paris, A Life of Mary Cassatt,*
New York: Farrar, Straus & Giroux, 1971.

ABOUT THE AUTHOR

Catherine Scheader was born in New York City where she studied English
literature and art at Hunter College and taught elementary school. After a move to
Monmouth County, New Jersey with her husband and three children, Mrs.
Scheader attended graduate school at Rutgers University and began to write
biographies for young people. Her first published series of books, *Proud Heritage,*
told the stories of five notable Black Americans. Mrs. Scheader has also written fic-
tion for children. Her own children, Barbara, John, and Susan, read all her
manuscripts and offer suggestions. Mrs. Scheader's husband is a deputy chief
engineer with the Department of Water Resources in New York City. Mrs.
Scheader is a reading specialist in the Marlboro Township public schools in New
Jersey.